The Shortest Way Home

A CONTEMPLATIVE PATH TO GOD

The Shortest Way Home

A CONTEMPLATIVE PATH TO GOD

WESLEY LACHMAN

O Street Publishing
Eugene, Oregon

Published by
O Street Publishing
3534 High Street
Eugene, Oregon 97405

Copyright © 2008 Wesley Rudolph Lachman.
All rights reserved.

The scripture quotations contained herein are from the New Revised Standard Version Bible, copyright © 1989 by the Division of Christian Education of the National Council of the Churches of Christ in the USA, and are used by permission. All rights reserved.

Book & cover design by Patricia Broersma,
greenhorsegraphics.com

Cover photograph courtesy of
Dayspring House of Prayer & Retreat,
Roberts Creek, British Columbia, Canada.

First paperback edition
Printed in the United States of America

ISBN 978-0-9791416-0-7
Library of Congress Control Number: 2007939895

Contents

Acknowledgments   vii

1. INTRODUCTION
Why the Contemplative Path?   1

2. SUFFERING & HAPPINESS
Why Walk a Spiritual Path?   9

3. BELIEF & EXPERIENCE
What Is the Basis of a Spiritual Life?   15

4. EXISTENCE & IMPERMANENCE
What Can I Really Count On?   21

5. BELONGING & SOCIAL CONVENTION
What Is Me and Mine?   29

6. SELF-CONCEPT & THE STORY OF I
Who Am I, Anyway?   35

7. THOUGHTS & REALITY
How Real Is Imagination?   41

8. SUFFERING & SELFLESSNESS
How Can I Be Released from Suffering?   55

9. FORMS & THE FORMLESS
Where Is God?   63

10. FULFILLMENT & EMPTINESS
How Do I Love?   71

11. MY SELF & DIVINE UNION
Where Is the Kingdom of God?   83

12. PRACTICE & GRACE
How Do I Walk This Path?   93

Notes   108

Bibliography   115

Acknowledgments

This book is the product of so many people that the reader may wonder if the author did anything more than put his name on the cover. First off, the spiritual community at Central Presbyterian Church, Eugene, Oregon graciously allowed me to develop this material by teaching several five-session courses on this spiritual path. Over a dozen students and friends took the trouble to critique the first complete draft. Several offered suggestions that significantly improved the book. I would especially like to thank the Rev. Joan Piersen, Dr. Michael Spezio, Dr. Edwin M. Good, Michele Bouche, Leonard Hockley, and the late Cary English.

All of the principal ideas herein are derived from the teachings of Joel Morwood, the Spiritual Director at the Center for Sacred Sciences, an interfaith community in Eugene where the mystical path is studied and practiced. Although Joel kindly critiqued portions of the manuscript, any mistakes must be laid at my door. The Center's excellent spiritual library of over 4,000 volumes has been an inexhaustible resource. My fellow spiritual seekers at the Center have been such loyal companions on the way.

This book also had able assistance from professionals in the world of print. Editor and writer Elizabeth Lyon was my friend and coach at many points along the way to publication. I took her classic book on nonfiction book proposals as my guide. Barbara Shaw provided an encouraging early line edit, while my book editor, Polly Bowman, found all the rough places and made the entire manuscript smooth and ready for the presses. As always, my wife and partner, Sharry, has been reading and supporting me all along the way.

1
INTRODUCTION

Why the Contemplative Path?

Our way to God was never intended to be obscure or complicated. This book is about a plain and simple path to God. It is plain because it is composed of our own uncluttered experience. We can see it in each moment of the daily round. In fact, our spiritual life can never be separate from the rest of life.

This path consists of a few simple steps. It is not a gaggle of complicated instructions or philosophical discourses. It is both plain and profound. Even a single word can be enough to direct your attention to where this path lies.

This contemplative path is such good news. If you begin to walk this path, your heart will love it. Your soul will rest peacefully in its embrace. Your spirit will literally take wings. Even your body will thank you for easing its burdens. It is a path that must be walked or practiced, and yet it leads to where you already are. *It is a journey from a place we have never been to a place we have never left.*[1] It can begin with some rational description such as found in this text, but the mystery of God is its true end.

This slim book is written for all those who desire a fresh, personal experience of God. Those who doubt their faith may find a wholly new way to a faith that cannot be doubted. Although written especially for Christians, it may well speak to others. If you feel dissatisfied with your day-to-day life and are looking for something deeper, it was written for you.

Origins of the path

Contemplative spirituality has been a significant emphasis within the Christian tradition from its earliest days. In our time, however, it is largely overlooked by mainstream Protestants and Catholics alike. Many of us have heard of contemplatives such as St. Augustine, St. Theresa of Avila, St. John of the Cross, Meister Eckhart, and Thomas Merton. But most of us have never heard even a brief description of the Christian path, or way to God, that they followed and taught.

As we shall see, there is good reason to believe that Jesus himself was a Jewish contemplative. Many passages in the letters of Paul are clearly contemplative. And from St. Anthony and the Desert Fathers in the third century until our own time, we have rarely been without some strong witnesses to this path. Since the monastics have, by and large, been the keepers of this tradition within Christianity, many contemporary Christians believe that one must withdraw from the world in order to engage in contemplative spiritual practices. And yet, it is reported that within local religious communities today there are growing numbers of ordinary laypeople and clergy who are practicing the contemplative path.

Awareness

"To contemplate" generally means to gaze attentively, to observe. In these pages, "contemplative" refers to one who is becoming aware of what is here and now, what just is. To put the same thing another way, *contemplative prayer is simply a wordless, trusting opening of self to the divine presence.*[2] The contemplative's concern is simply to be aware of what is actually going on, in contrast to thinking about it or getting lost in a train of thought. This is a simple idea, but not easy to do, since we live in our thoughts most of the time without realizing it.

Sometimes the word "mystical" is used in place of "contemplative" to refer to this path. This word points to the mystery of God. "Mystery" originally meant "closed," or "mute," implying that nothing can really be said. Contemplatives emphasize that God can be experienced but cannot be either rationally known or verbally described. Thomas Merton wrote about trying to communicate the contemplative experience:

> *It can be suggested by words, by symbols, but in the very moment of trying to indicate what it knows the contemplative mind takes back what it has said, and denies what it has affirmed.*[3]

The contemplative path to God takes two principal forms that are completely compatible with each other: the path of devotion and the path of wisdom. The devotional path seeks to love God so completely that one's self is given up and only a divine union remains. The path of wisdom seeks so ardently to find the truth about self and God that all falsehood falls away and only divine union remains. It is the wisdom path, the search for truth, that we will focus upon in this book. This focus will take the form of a series of inquiries into our concrete experience. As we move along this path of inquiry, however, it is our devotion that will enable us to persevere.

Limits and possibilities

This book is intended to provide a brief introduction to this oft-neglected way to God. Since it covers many of the principal contemplative themes in a brief format, it can present only a very limited treatment of each. You may experience it as something akin to being introduced to someone at a dinner party: "And this is Laura, who is a graphic designer and was a volunteer in Kenya for several years," and then Laura is seated at the other end of a long table. You do get introduced, but if you really want to get to know Laura, you will have to sit down with her over coffee at a later time. I hope this book will provide introduction enough for you to decide if you want to learn to walk this path. The last chapter and the bibliography contain suggestions as to how you might proceed.

Contemplatives say that their knowledge of God cannot be rationally described. Their path *to* God, however, can indeed be logically and rationally described. This is our aim here: to show the

a contemplative path to God

credibility of this incredible path. Please note that each chapter builds upon the one that precedes it. If you find yourself uncertain as to what the basis for such-and-such could be, the preceding chapter may provide some clues.

Many paths

No spiritual approach can rightly claim to be the best for everyone. Many paths and many teachers have been provided so that everyone might find God. However, for some of us, the contemplative path opens up spiritual depths that we could not have imagined in our mainstream Christian life. For example, the contemplatives teach that we are mistaken about who we think we are, and this is the cause of our suffering and dissatisfaction. They say that we are wrapped up in our own ideas in such a way that we cannot see the deep truth that cannot be expressed as an idea.

Let us begin, then, at the very beginning of what this path has to teach us. Why would anyone enter a spiritual path? Surely there are more entertaining activities, easier roads to take, avenues that offer more in the way of the possessions, power, and prestige that everyone seems to desire.

2
SUFFERING & HAPPINESS

Why Walk a Spiritual Path?

We set out on a spiritual path because our sense of sin has made us dissatisfied or despairing, both of which are forms of suffering. Some may take sin to refer to a moral or legal matter. However, beneath all our should-nots and guilt feelings about sin lies a fractured relation with God. This foundational separation must result in suffering, for it means that we have left our true home and true self, believing that enduring happiness is to be found elsewhere. We may not be aware of this relationship between our suffering and our separation from God. We may simply feel deeply unhappy with how our life has turned out. Or, more subtly, we may experience the suffering of being separated from the fulfillment of some of our deepest needs and desires. And so we reach out for some kind of help. Isn't it ironic that our sin and separation from God are seemingly just the gift we need in order to begin our spiritual path.

Not entirely happy

Those who are well have no need of a physician, but those who are sick. I have come to call not the righteous, but sinners.[4] If you are one of *those who are well* and feeling no pain, you are unlikely to set forth to seek Jesus' help. And if you see yourself as already *righteous,* it may be difficult to open yourself to Christ's call to a deeper life. We all have a great tendency to remain where we are comfortable, even in a cozy chair. So it is that virtually every spiritual path begins with suffering. If we are entirely happy there is no reason to look

a contemplative path to God

for something else. *Truly I tell you, it will be hard for a rich person to enter the kingdom of God.*[5] And if we do feel totally happy, have we unwittingly spun a cocoon around ourselves and blocked out the pain and suffering of the world?

Inward focus

Every Christian path begins with suffering and a saving experience of God. Then we set out to follow Christ. Most of us tend to focus outwardly, toward God as infinitely beyond us. However, the contemplatives maintain an inward focus wherein God is increasingly revealed as we discover more of ourselves. They suggest that no matter where we search in all the world we will never find anything so close to God as our own true self, right here, created in God's image. They recall Jesus' promise to be within us and St. Paul's exhortation, *Do you not know that you are God's temple and that God's Spirit dwells in you?*[6] Thus St. Augustine prays, *Let me know myself, Lord, and I will know You.*[7]

There is certainly nothing that can so eclipse our relation with God as holding onto a false sense of who we are. As the anonymous author of the Christian classic *The Cloud of Unknowing* warns us: *Long after you have successfully forgotten every creature and its works, you will find that a naked knowing and feeling of your own being still remains between you and your God.*[8]

Thus the first step on the contemplative path is just to acknowledge our desire not to suffer, our yearning for something better. The second step is to begin to experiment with drawing closer to our God, our Happiness, by exploring someone made in God's image—us! As we take these steps, we will find ourselves drawn away from mere thoughts about God and drawn toward encountering the living God in our own experience.

Don't take my word for it

Contemplative teachers remind their students not to believe anything they are taught, but rather to test it in their own experience. When we have seen and heard something for ourselves, we have gone beyond hearsay. After all, I cannot have my own experience of God merely by hearing you de-

a contemplative path to God

scribe yours. Therefore, in the following exercise and subsequent ones, you will be invited to test what you have read by looking into your own experience. These experiments in honest looking will inevitably be the deepest part of this book.

You find out

> Examine your own experience to see if what you have just read is true. For example, do you find that you try to move away from situations that cause you suffering and toward those that promise happiness for you and others? What role does your desire for happiness play in your motivation for walking your religious path?

3
BELIEF & EXPERIENCE

What Is the Basis of a Spiritual Life?

When they begin to explore who they are, the first thing contemplatives encounter is their experience of life. From the first light of morning until nodding off to sleep, everything in life appears to them within their conscious experience or awareness. Yet many of us think that the first thing is that we believe something. We believe in Christ, we believe in God, we believe in the Bible as the God-inspired story of our faith. How could anything be more basic than that?

A finger pointing

Contemplative Christians base their spiritual life more upon their immediate, examined experience than upon any particular belief. After all, beliefs are meant to point us toward something that is real. They have little value sitting in our heads as mere thoughts. They guide our spiritual path only if they help us move toward the reality they point to. *In short, a religious belief is only a finger pointing to the moon. Some religious people never get beyond the study of the finger.*[9] Contemplatives encourage us to consciously experience walking the path indicated by our beliefs. As we walk, God will guide us in and through our experience.

It is within our experience that everything appears to us, including the experience of God. Sights and sounds, sensations and thoughts, even dreams arise only in our conscious experience. This awareness is all we have to go on. Our beliefs themselves take form there. No authentic spiritual way can exist apart from what appears in our awareness. Therefore, contemplatives pay careful attention to their own experience as a guide for the next step on their path. Whatever they decide, it always comes out of their experience. Their conscious experience is the foundation of their life and path. *Very truly, I tell you, we speak of what we know and testify to what we have seen.*[10]

Dead belief

Belief in God through Christ is our beginning for this Christian contemplative path and points to the presence of God in human form. Jesus clearly taught that he and God would be in our hearts. So contemplatives begin to look for the divine in their own human lives. To the Letter of James, which says, *So faith by itself, if it has no works, is dead,*[11] the contemplative would add that belief by itself, if it is without experience, is dead. Contemplatives desire to taste the mysterious presence of God, to whom our Christian beliefs are pointing.

For the purposes of our journey in this book, it will be helpful if you stay aware of your religious beliefs as beliefs, as thoughts. Eventually some may be challenged, and others may be expanded "beyond belief." You will need only one simple belief: that you can trust your own direct experience of life. This means to first trust your own awareness to convey reality to you before rushing in with beliefs, analysis, opinions and thoughts in order to "improve" the reality that God has given. This trust will be put to good use in the next chapter as we look at a contemplative experience of the ordinary objects of everyday life.

a contemplative path to God

You find out

Try this thought experiment: Imagine that a close friend is out of touch in a far-off place. Since you cannot observe the friend directly, you can only believe that your friendship still exists. Then imagine that an air ticket arrives in the mail. You have an opportunity to visit your friend and experience your friendship directly. Would you exchange the experience for the belief? As you look back, what has been the best way for you to build relationships, by belief or by direct experience? What role does belief play?

4
EXISTENCE & IMPERMANENCE

What Can You Really Count On?

Let us now go further into conscious experience with our contemplative friends. We can take another step on this path by paying close attention to the objects that God has placed in our everyday life. At first glance, it appears obvious that they are simply there: mountains, cats, automobiles, newspapers. They all show up in our conscious experience, don't they? As contemporary Christians, we think of all this wondrous physical world as originally created by God and that we have made all sorts of things out of that original creation. We don't ordinarily question our belief that the things in our life have a solid, permanent, separate existence.

The disappearing cup

However, when contemplatives observe the amazing reality of a mountain or a cat, their *immediate* experience is that things do not have an independent, continuous existence of their own. By "immediate" experience they mean the direct, raw experience of the senses without naming things, without telling ourselves anything about what is going on, without thinking. Raw experience indicates that everything is impermanent.

Let me try to illustrate. Suppose you are reading a book and drinking a cup of coffee in a coffee shop. You put down the book, pick up the cup to drink, and the book suddenly disappears from your visual consciousness. Put down the cup and pick up the book and the cup disappears. Walk out through the doorway and the whole coffee shop

a contemplative path to God

disappears. Everything is constantly appearing in or disappearing from our awareness. Contemplatives point out that this happens constantly to sights, sounds, sensations, smells, tastes, and thoughts. We hear a bird chirp. The sound is there, then gone. We have a bodily pain, it changes. We have a thought, it goes. In our moment-by-moment experience of them, all things are impermanent. They arise in and dissolve into our consciousness. James Finley, an outstanding student of Thomas Merton, puts it so well: *And we see that this not lasting quality of the present moment is the way the present moment always is. And in seeing this, we see the permanence of impermanence.*[12]

You will probably object that the cup does not really disappear when you pick up the book, that we know it is there and that is why we can return to it. But our "knowing" that the cup is there is actually a belief which we take to be true while the cup is hidden by the book. Our "knowing" about the cup is exposed as a (mistaken) belief when we are engrossed in our book, a waiter removes our cup, and we reach for the cup that is not there.

This suggests that what we think we know is more impermanent than we realize. We think we know where things are and what they are. But apart from direct experience, this thinking represents only belief or thought, which may be grossly inaccurate.

It takes a universe

Perhaps you have another objection to this idea of impermanence. You will admit that our knowledge can be pretty shaky. You will grant that sights, sounds, sensations, thoughts, are constantly changing for us—that is, for our perception. But surely all those objects that we see out there are really independent and exist in themselves. That cup is probably out in the kitchen being washed.

First, contemplatives say, the things out there are not permanent and independent at all. They all depend upon the myriad causes and decisions that brought each one into existence. For example, our coffee cup's existence is dependent upon thousands and millions of people who conceived of it, experimented with ways of designing and creating it, engineered and operated manufacturing plants, distributed and sold it, as well as the ancillary industries which provided the machines and shelter, and those who provided all the social and political infrastructure in which all these developments could take place, as well as the appropriate environment supporting life and health, which itself was supported by the earth and its relative stability in relation to the rest of the universe. Upon examination, it takes a universe to make a cup. Each individual thing is resting upon the Whole Thing. *God created the heavens and the earth*. Not a single thing has an independent existence.

Days like grass

Another telling point against the independent existence of things is that nothing remains what it is, even for a second. Everything is in transition. Each thing is in the process of wearing out and fading away, *where moth and rust consume and where thieves break in and steal.*[13] In ten years the cup will likely be broken, or worn out or lost. If the scientists tell us that Mt. Everest is gradually wearing down, how much more that stately tree or your aging auto. Our experience tells us that everything is impermanent. And of course, each of us is impermanent also. *As for mortals, their days are like grass; they flourish like a flower of the field; for the wind passes over it, and it is gone, and its place knows it no more.*[14] Some of us will be gone before the tree, some before the cup.

Why this concern with the impermanence of everything? When we begin to see that literally everything is passing away moment by moment, we find that some of our assumptions about ourselves and God begin to unravel. In this next chapter we will see that this is particularly true for our possessions.

a contemplative path to God

You find out

Take a few minutes to experience impermanence: Walk across the room or down the street. Notice how the world is constantly changing as it flows past. Things get larger, then disappear. Sounds arise and dissolve. You turn your head to look at something, and dozens of other things drop from view. Then pause to look at something growing, a house plant or a tree. Let your mind go back to when it was just a seed cradled in another plant. Let your mind go forward; this growing thing will have its end. Is everything in your life impermanent?

5
BELONGING & SOCIAL CONVENTION

What Is Me and Mine?

As Christians we commonly think of some of these impermanent, transitory things as belonging to us as individuals: our clothing, our books and papers, our furniture, our automobile, and so on. True, we may occasionally remind ourselves that we are merely the stewards or overseers of everything that God has given into our care. But in daily life we behave as if these things are ours.

If we look more deeply, however, we can become aware that we own nothing. Since everything is impermanent and transitory, there is no such thing as a possession. Our belongings appear and disappear in our awareness moment by moment. We misplace them and cannot remember where we put them. We cannot hold onto them even in our minds. Eventually each of us will be finally separated by loss, by deterioration, by death, from literally everything that we call "mine." Everything is impermanent, so nothing can be possessed.

Imaginary ownership

Even before a final separation, it can be shown that no object actually belongs to you. We may say that your fingers belong to your hand, for they are attached to it, and only you can make them move. But your bicycle or automobile does not belong to you in that way. If we were to directly experience your automobile in this moment (without imposing any concepts upon it), we could see that you are not physically connected to it any more than I am. It is not a part of who you are at all. And if I should drive your automobile, it will respond to me just as it would to you. It does not perform according

a contemplative path to God

to any special relationship.

We do indeed have a social convention called "ownership." This is an imaginary relationship between you and your belongings. We agree as a society to imagine that there is a special link between you and your "property." This imaginary link helps us maintain order in our society and resolve questions about who has the legal right to use what property. So the idea of property belonging to someone plays an important role. But it is still only a thought, a piece of imagination. The contemplative says "In reality, nothing belongs to me." The contemplative walks a path of poverty.

Recognizing our poverty is a key turning point on our contemplative journey. Anthony de Mello, a mystic from India, says that possessions can even determine whether or not we can find the kingdom of God. He states that it is both easy and difficult to find the kingdom:

> *Easy because it is all around you and within you, and all you have to do is reach out and take possession of it.*

> *Difficult because if you wish to possess the kingdom you may possess nothing else.*[15]

Less than nothing

Perhaps now we are able to appreciate why Jesus and so many of the holy ones embraced poverty. Often they practiced external poverty, but this always represented an internal poverty. St. Paul, for example, says:

> *I regard everything as loss because of the surpassing value of knowing Christ Jesus my Lord. For his sake I have suffered the loss of all things, and I regard them as rubbish, in order that I may gain Christ.*[16]

St. John of the Cross takes this one step further as he warns that in relation to God all created things can be *less* than nothing:

A person's attachments to creatures [created things] are less than nothing since these attachments are an impediment to and deprive the soul of transformation in God—just as darkness is nothing and less than nothing since it is a privation of light. One who is in darkness does not comprehend the light, so neither will a person attached to [created things] be able to comprehend God.[17]

Indeed, how can we give our total allegiance to God—heart, soul, mind, and strength—if we insist upon withholding our personal possessions from the bargain? And how did we ever delude ourselves into thinking we could find lasting happiness in our possessions when we are losing every one of them? In the next chapter we will continue to move toward the truth of ourselves and of God by looking beyond our fantasy of ownership.

You find out

See if what we have been saying about possessions is confirmed by your own experience: Look at one of your everyday belongings. For a few moments disregard any thoughts you have about it, and simply experience it and yourself. What do you observe? How are you actually connected with this object? Now look at a second object that does not belong to you. Is there any difference between the two in how you are connected?

6
SELF-CONCEPT & THE STORY OF I

Who Am I, Anyway?

As we continue to examine those who are made in God's image, the contemplatives ask us to shift our focus. Thus far we have been looking at our experience of the world, but now we turn our attention to our experience of our self: *Who am I?* Listen to St. Teresa of Avila as she exhorts her sisters on this point:

> *It is no small pity, and should cause us no little shame, that, through our own fault, we do not understand ourselves, or*

> *know who we are ... and only know that we are living in these bodies, and have a vague idea, because we have heard it and because our Faith tells us so, that we possess souls.*[18]

Each of us has a concept of who we think we are. We regard this self-concept as a very personal thing. It belongs to us and to no one else. We think no one else really knows who we are. We would be surprised to know how much energy we spend evaluating our self-concept and trying to improve it.

How much of me is me?

Our path now turns toward this self-concept. Impressed with the realization that nothing belongs to them, contemplatives inquire: If I really possess nothing at all, then what or who is this self? Who am I? Perhaps my relationships can tell me who I am: My occupation certainly helps to define me in society, but if I lose my job, still here I am. My friends and family are crucial to who I am. Yet,

a contemplative path to God

when one of them dies, I am still here. I will be grieving, but I have not become someone else. My own body seems part of who I am, but if I lose a leg in an auto accident, I will not thereby become another person. So apparently none of these relationships can define who I am, not even my relation to my own body.

If nothing external will answer the question of who we are, the contemplatives invite us to look inward. What do we find there? We find sensations from different parts of the body, memories and anticipations, a variety of feelings and emotions about what is going on with us, and various thoughts about this and that. But what we had hoped to encounter—our identity, a self, some kind of answer to "who am I?"—we do not find. We certainly do not find a little person sitting up somewhere in our head, pulling levers to operate our mouth and arms and legs like a heavy equipment operator sitting up in his little cab. What we do find running around inside is the idea that we are a self. But this is the same self-concept that we set out to investigate in the first place.

The story of I

An examination of this self-concept reveals it is what the name implies: a self-centered collection of thoughts and emotions about "me." It is not static; it is impermanent. It is not something I can possess. For, while I remain the same *whatever-I-really-am* year after year, my self-concept changes day-by-day, moment-by-moment. First I am depressed; afterwards I feel good. Then I am sad, then anxious, then proud. This swirl of "I" thoughts keeps itself alive by constantly talking to itself about what is going on with me: "Well, I sure have a lot to do today. I'm worried about finding a present for Jerry's birthday, but I guess I can find something at the drugstore on my way to the market. Gee, I can't seem to get my hair to lie down right. I look like a freak. Oops, I'm going to be late for the meeting. I hate to come in late ..." Some such story is chatting along inside everyone, telling who "I" am, how "I" see the world, and how "I" am going to handle the challenges it presents. Thomas Merton explains why we do this:

a contemplative path to God

I wind experiences around myself and cover myself with pleasures and glory like bandages in order to make myself perceptible to myself and to the world, as if I were an invisible body that could only become visible when something visible covered its surface.[19]

We are inevitably the protagonist, the star of this continuous story. It's all about me; it's the *story of I*.[20] Contemplatives teach that this ephemeral story is the only individual "self" that we will ever find. Many names have been given to this: little self, external self, conditioned self, false self, egoic consciousness—to name a few. We assume that this is who we actually are, for any alternative we think of can only be more thoughts, more of the story. Merton calls this *an illusory person, a false self.* He goes on to assert that such a self cannot have any real existence, *because God does not know anything about [it]. And to be unknown of God is altogether too much privacy.*[21]

In the next chapter we must consider how the

story of I operates in our daily life and its crucial role on the contemplative path to God.

You find out

> Listen to what your own *story of I* sounds like: Look up from your reading for a minute or two. Just let your eyes rest quietly on the floor or the wall. Wait until several thoughts have arisen in your mind, and watch them. What do these thoughts have in common? Who or what is at the center of the little stories that these thoughts are telling? And here is another experiment: The next time you watch a good video, note what happens to your *story of I*.

7
THOUGHTS & REALITY

How Real Is Imagination?

Contemplatives bear witness to the fact that we all have the same problem with our thoughts and stories: we take them to be real. In fact, thoughts can seem so real to us that they easily overshadow what is actually here and now. Although we are seated at the dinner table, in our imagination we are still in a lively argument at the coffee shop. We drive across town but miss our turnoff while we are thinking about tonight's event. We are reading the newspaper and do not hear someone speaking to us right across the breakfast table. And surely we have all had the experience of having the room reappear when we return from being lost in thought. We can fail to notice what is happening right in front of us when our attention has been captured by our imagination.

One result of this tendency to live in our thoughts is that we almost never encounter another human being. Instead, we encounter our thoughts about them. We assume that we already know who they are. If they say something surprising, we may respond to our quick reflection about being surprised. If they appear to insult us, we react to our interior story and feelings about being insulted instead of to the person standing before us. We tend to see everything through a veil of thought. How can we get beyond this veil to what is really there?

Real, but imaginary

C. S. Lewis says that *everything is real. The proper question is "A real what?", e.g., a real snake or a real delirium tremens?*[22] Like objects in

a contemplative path to God

a dream, our thoughts appear to be quite realistic when we are caught up in them. Imaginatively, in our mind, we *are* in them. These internal images can draw our attention away from our perceptions to such a degree that these images seem to be our actual environment. However, no matter how much they may absorb our attention, our thoughts are not real in the same way that, for example, a glass of water is real. Rather, thoughts are real bits of imagination; they are imaginary by nature. They are mental images of sensations, sights, sounds, and so on. You can fully imagine that you are drinking a glass of cool spring water. It can seem quite real. But when you are done, you are still thirsty.

An everyday trance

The mind's job is to produce thoughts. It is almost impossible to stop it. Our entire Western culture lives in its head, entranced with its thoughts. We are so accustomed to thinking about everything that at first it may be difficult to notice the difference between our actual experience and our experience overlaid with thought. We may believe we are just looking, for example, at a garden in the spring. But if we pay attention we will find that we are compulsively overlaying our perceptions with thought: "Hmm, plenty of green here, red roses. Oh! Some orange! Nice shady place over there, bright impatiens. Ugh, dandelion." However, with practice, it is possible to become more aware of our habit of constant thinking about what we see. We can learn to let our thoughts drift by without getting lost in them and, finally, to see the garden in its own unique and divine glory.

Knowing thyself

Almost all our thoughts form part of the continuing flow of imagination that we named the *story of I* in the last chapter. Contemplatives endeavor to discover just exactly what is this *story of I* that represents who they think they are. Most practice meditation, learning to observe thoughts as they arise in awareness, remain for a while, and then just dissolve into nothing. They see the thoughts composing the *story of I* arise and melt away just like any other thoughts. *The story of I*

a contemplative path to God

is imaginary, composed entirely of mental images. St. Catherine of Siena hears God say, *In self knowledge, then, thou wilt humble thyself; seeing that, in thyself, thou dost not even exist.*[23]

No self at all

Now the importance of seeing the impermanence of all things becomes clear. Literally everything in our lives comes and goes, is born and dies, is in constant change. So what is the unchanging presence that has been seeing this? Who is this watcher? Who is the one who has been looking out at the world all these many years? Who are we?

At this point we encounter what may well be the most central teaching of the contemplative path: selflessness. This is not a moral selflessness, putting our personal needs to one side in order to help someone else. It is not even the sacrificial selflessness that gives up one's life to save another. Rather, it is the unbelievable selflessness of not having an individual self at all.

This is in dramatic contrast to the wisdom of this world. Our parents, our teachers, our peers, our culture have all taught us that we exist, that we need to stand up for ourselves, develop ourselves, make something of ourselves, take care of ourselves, and so on. Self-improvement is a huge industry in the U.S.

The contemplatives invite us to something different, echoing St. Paul: *Do not be conformed to this world, but be transformed by the renewing of your minds.*[24] They invite us to observe in our own experience that within our physical bodies there is nothing more than thoughts of a self, *in thyself, thou dost not even exist*. These thoughts about self are real thoughts, but they are pointing to something that exists only in the imagination, like a unicorn. We live in the illusion that they point to something real. No matter how hard we look, there is nothing within us that we could call our self. In reality there is only one true self, the self of God. Jesus prayed that we might realize this: *The glory that you have given me I have given them, so that they may be one, as we are one, I in them and you in me, that they may become completely one.*[25] The self of God is indeed within us all, but that is

a contemplative path to God

not our individual self. So this is the astounding secret of the mystics and contemplatives: that we are, in fact, selfless. This selflessness is already here. It is not a goal to be achieved but rather a reality to be discovered.

Take a look

This is indeed a revolutionary teaching. If you are surprised or appalled, fearful or confused, that may be a good thing. For then perhaps you have heard the teaching. You may think that it is false, or that it is true, but all our opinions are secondary to the reality of selflessness. The question is: What do you see in your own direct experience of yourself? Don't merely conform to what others have told you —*be transformed by the renewing of your minds*. What do you actually observe?

Enjoying the story

Some will object: What about the gift of my individuality? My personality? My unique purpose? Are all these to be thrown aside as so much fantasy? Not at all. When we see that our *story of I* is simply a story, it becomes delightful. Who doesn't enjoy a good story? Like a motion picture, our story has sadness, joy, struggle, and final resolution. We can watch and enjoy all of this thoroughly. And isn't it the imaginary characters in our life who make our story so fascinating? What would life be without them? Once we see clearly that each of us is playing an imaginary character, everyone we encounter has a role to play in our daily human drama. We lose our compulsive interest in our "self" and gain an appreciation for all the diverse roles in the drama of life. Each is an expression of the whole. *Now you are the body of Christ and individually members of it.*[26]

The blessing of selflessness

All of this has vital relevance for the question of suffering. Contemplatives point out that our suffering arises when we take the thoughts of our *story of I* to be real. When my *story of I* is threatened—which occurs often—I believe that there is a real self in danger and, therefore, I begin to suffer. When my ego-story thinks that certain

a contemplative path to God

people or things belong to me, I suffer, for I am uncertain as to whether or not I can keep them safe from harm. I am afraid of the pain of loss. The vast majority of my life energy is spent in defending or enhancing this ego, this *story of I*. Like a small bird in a vast forest, my story has to search constantly for nourishment to keep it going and to maintain a watchful eye for the many enemies who would do it harm.

I feel better, so much better, since I laid my burdens down the old gospel song declares. And contemplatives can say "Amen!" to that. What a burden of suffering it is to have to spend every waking hour evaluating, protecting, developing, enhancing, promoting our self. What a blessed relief to see that it is all just thought. Once we realize that our "self" is a work of imagination like a poem or a painting, we can stop taking our *story of I* so seriously. We can watch our thoughts of self chase each other around for a while and not be disturbed in the slightest. What freedom! What release! What salvation! Jesus taught for this: *so that my joy may be in you, and that your joy may be complete.*[27] It is like awakening from a terrible nightmare to discover the light of day streaming in the window. *You have stripped off the old self with its practices and have clothed yourselves with the new self, which is being renewed in knowledge according to the image of its Creator.*[28]

I like this, I hate that

Until we see that our self is imaginary—not just read or think about it, but *see* it—we will continue to suffer from our *story of I*. We can start becoming more aware if we pay attention to the judgments we make each day. For it is our everyday likes and dislikes that reinforce the *story of I* and make it seem real. On a cold day, you have a hot cup of mocha java. You think, "Wow. I really like this." The thought is not only that there is this great taste and warmth, this pleasure. The thought also includes this "I," this entity, that is having the pleasure. Or when you look at the disagreeable task of talking to a friend about money, you think, "I don't want to do this." Again there is the sense of discomfort, but also the sense that there is

a contemplative path to God

this real, substantial "I" who wants to avoid this conversation. The next time you make a judgment, take a hard look at this "I" and see that it is only a thought.

The more we rehearse our opinions to ourselves and to others without noticing that they are just thoughts, the more real they seem. Therefore, the more real our self seems as their author. The thoughts seem to say to one another, "I have lots of likes and dislikes," generating yet another thought, "I am real!" But these thoughts are imaginary.

Staying alive

Since the *story of I* is composed of mental images, it disappears when these thoughts and images die down. In the midst of dreamless sleep, our *story of I* disappears completely. So, in order to keep itself alive during our waking hours, our story keeps a veritable swarm of likes and dislikes going: "I like this, I hate that, I wish he would go away, I am dreading this, this is so good, I have a strong opinion about that, I would like to avoid this, I think she is so terrific." Again, these opinions are simply thoughts. These likes and dislikes cannot be found anywhere out in the real world, for they are imaginary. You may like your car, but your liking is an image floating in your mind. It is not a part of the car itself. Our likes and dislikes are imaginary. So we can begin to loosen up a bit, and take our opinions less seriously. They can sometimes be important, but they will always be imaginary.

In the next chapter we will look at how awareness of our true nature can release us from the suffering in our life.

a contemplative path to God

You find out

Observe how your own judgments operate: As you go about your planned activities during the day, spend some time noticing your judgments about what you encounter: good or bad, desirable or undesirable. Now select an opinion to examine. State your judgment forcefully to yourself. What happens to your sense of self, your *story of I?* Then look at your opinion. What is it? What are your likes and dislikes made up of?

8
SUFFERING & SELFLESSNESS

How Can I Be Released from Suffering?

We suffer from losing what we wanted to keep and getting stuck with what we wanted to be rid of. We suffer from not getting to possess what we want and from the fear that we will have to deal with what we do not like. Can we recognize this as idolatry, the belief that some particular thing or person is necessary for our happiness—that God is not enough for us? And then can we see that our suffering is due, not to our pain, but to our refusal to accept what God has given us to deal with in this moment?

Two ways to guarantee suffering

There are two aspects to this suffering. One is a focus upon the thing that is liked or disliked: "I have lost *this object*. I will never be able to replace *this*." This friend or event or thing was so important. The second aspect concerns who is doing the liking or disliking: "*I* have lost this object. *I* am so unhappy." *I* had identified with this object as something of *mine*, under *my* control, part of *my* life. When the object is gone, my sense of self is diminished, part of me is cut away, and I am the less for this. But I have set myself up for this suffering by believing that some of my identity and happiness depend upon this object.

Hobbes, the cartoon character, watching little Calvin choke and cough from his first cigarette, turns toward the reader and comments, "You'd think this would be an easy habit to break." Similarly, you would think that this habit of causing our own suffering would be an easy habit to

a contemplative path to God

break. In fact, it is difficult only because we fail to pay careful attention to what is happening. For example, suppose one day we realize that we are very uncomfortable at a party but cannot determine why. We cast about for the source of our discomfort and finally notice that the beautiful sweater we have chosen especially for this occasion is also a very heavy sweater, and the room temperature is about 80 degrees. Once we notice this, we have three choices: One, we can decide to let go of our desire to be comfortable and so end our fretting and suffering about it. Two, if we are willing to forgo wearing our beautiful sweater, it is a simple matter to remove the sweater and end our suffering. Three, we can continue to wear the sweater while desiring to be cooler—that is, we can choose to continue to suffer.

Letting things go

The two aspects of our suffering—suffering over the object and suffering about the self—correspond to two ways of releasing our suffering.

The first way is to stop clinging to the specific

things that are causing us to suffer, like the sweater. Remember Jesus' parable of the rich man: *You fool! This very night your life is being demanded of you. And the things you have prepared, whose will they be?*[29] When suffering, look for what you are refusing to give up (clinging to having it) or what you are trying to get rid of (clinging to not having it). Look for what you want to possess or what you are trying to avoid. Recall the teaching that all things are impermanent, that you really don't possess this thing, anyway. Then, when you discover what you are clinging to, you have the option of ending your suffering by letting go of it. You can even declare to yourself, "I admit that I never owned this thing. I refuse to tie my happiness to it. I accept the reality of this situation as it is right now."

Letting go in this context does not mean throwing the thing away or giving it to a friend. It means letting go of all thoughts that this belongs to you or is identified with you. It means entering into a deep internal poverty. This letting go means to cease fighting with the One who gives us our real situation right now. We may wish it were different, but we can still accept reality. *Father, if you are willing, remove this cup from me; yet, not my will but yours be done.*[30]

Letting yourself go

The second way to release our suffering is to look at the one who is experiencing it. You can begin by noticing once again that you are not so permanent and solid as your thoughts have been telling you. Be open to seeing afresh whether every last thing in your life is passing away, moment by moment. Even your ego, your *story of I*, is nothing more than an ever changing story. There really isn't anything substantial about who you think you are. When this becomes clear, you can begin to inquire within, "Who is suffering here, anyway?"

Richard Rohr, a Franciscan, likes to speak of the necessity of becoming poor, of letting go of all our possessions. But it is the self, the *story of I*, that gives the most difficulty:

> *The issue isn't primarily material goods,*
> *but our spiritual and intellectual goods,*

> *my ego, my reputation, my self-image, my need to be right, my need to be successful, my need to have everything under control, my need to be loved.*[31]

Spacious awareness

Contemplatives are unanimous in their testimony that your true nature is the space of consciousness in which your *story of I*, and everything else in life, appears for a time and then dissolves. We are not our thoughts; we are the space of awareness in which our thoughts appear. Douglas Harding, a grand old English gentleman, likes to point out this odd fact: If you simply observe without thinking about it, your immediate experience is that on your shoulders, where other people have a head, you have the whole world of sight and sound. At the center of "you" is this spacious capacity for the whole universe of sight, sound, sensation, and thought. Everything in awareness is yours, in the sense of being in your consciousness. But no one thing or person or sensation belongs to your consciousness more than any other. No special

a contemplative path to God

thread of possession connects you with any one set of objects in contrast to any other set. Your consciousness reflects everything impartially—good, bad or ugly—like a mirror does. Since your empty awareness does not play favorites, you can appreciate literally everything without getting "stuck" on anything. Everything is within awareness but nothing can be affixed to it. And every thing is passing away, including the ideas in your *story of I*.

Since there is no way for your empty space of awareness to hang onto anything, you can stop trying. There is no need to get rid of any of your things or relationships. Just see through the illusion that they are yours or you. Appreciate them for what they are instead of as something to make you safer or more important. Begin to look past the thoughts in the *story of I* and into the spaciousness in which they float, and your suffering will subside.

You find out

What is your experience of suffering over an object and about your self? Think of some person or thing or circumstance that was important to you but that has been taken from you recently. Remember the pain of losing this, and stay with that feeling for a minute. Then let go of the feeling. As it recedes, recognize that it is impermanent. See that it does not belong to what you are. Then observe yourself. What is the story you are telling yourself about this loss? What words are you using? Leaving the story aside for a moment, look for the one who has suffered this loss.

9
FORMS & THE FORMLESS

Where Is God?

As we become more aware of this spacious consciousness that is the essence of who we are, we come closer to God. Brother Lawrence, who worked daily with God in a monastery kitchen, reported: *I renounced, for the love of Him, everything that was not He, and I began to live as if there was none but He and I in the world.*[32] We too can start to let go of everything, refuse to pretend that we possess any person, thing, or situation. How would such a path help us to encounter God in a new way?

Draw me nearer

One helpful image is provided by Huston Smith, author of the classic *The World's Religions*. He suggests that we can speak of God with form or God without form. When we Christians speak of God the Father, we are speaking of God without form: the unsearchable, unfathomable one who may be encountered but never explained. In fact, in our tradition it is expressly forbidden to give God a form. *You shall not make for yourself an idol, whether in the form of anything that is in heaven above, or that is on the earth beneath, or that is in the water under the earth.*[33] We worship the mysterious God who is infinitely beyond any description or imagined form. As St. Thomas Aquinas put it so crisply: *We do not know what God is.*

Contemplatives point out that when our minds are focused upon the *story of I* and all its likes and dislikes, it is impossible to see God the Father, who cannot be equated with any of these things. As the great 13th century contemplative Meister Eckhart said, *One image can block out all of God.* But we can start to move our attention away from our thoughts and more toward the space of our awareness in which thoughts float. As we do so, we see that consciousness is open to everything because it has no form of its own to interfere with anything. Since it has no form, it cannot have any walls or boundaries. It has room for every sight, sound, sensation, and thought that may arise. Everything we experience takes shape within the space of consciousness and disappears again into consciousness. When we learn to be aware of this formless spaciousness, we will begin to experience the infinite spaciousness and formlessness of the Father. Indeed, can we say where our emptiness ends and the emptiness of God begins?

Our Lord in form

In Jesus the Christ our Lord we encounter God *with* form. *The Word became flesh and lived among us, and we have seen his glory, the glory as of a father's only son, full of grace and truth.*[34] The gospel stories of Jesus invite us to see the glory of God walking and speaking in this man. We imagine him. We see an actual form in our mind. We are called to follow the teaching and example of our savior, this God-with-form. With him we learn to die to our old self. Because he has the form of a human being, it is possible to direct our worship and adoration toward this Jesus of the gospels, this Christ of faith. More than that, we can participate in this form, we can actually re-present this form in the form of our bodies: *Now you are the body of Christ and individually members of it.*[35]

Mother Teresa of Calcutta recognized the form of our Lord in others. She saw him in the faces of filthy, rejected people dying on the sidewalks of Calcutta. Contemplatives teach that the risen Christ comes to all of us through others, but are we too preoccupied with our thoughts to see him?

Blowing in the wind

The Holy Spirit is the principal worship focus for some branches of the Christian church and largely ignored in others. For most of us, the Spirit does not play as great a role as the Father and the Son. One interesting exception is the traditional Quaker meeting, where members sit in silence, let-

a contemplative path to God

ting go of their thoughts and words, until someone feels moved by the Spirit to speak to the group. This is akin to the contemplative practice of meditation, wherein the meditator allows thoughts to come and go without focusing attention on them, so that the formless Spirit beyond thought might be encountered.

It is striking that the word used to denote "Spirit" in both Old and New Testaments is the word for "breath" or "wind." The breath or wind of God is beyond our rational understanding. *The wind blows where it chooses, and you hear the sound of it, but you do not know where it comes from or where it goes. So it is with everyone who is born of the Spirit.*[36] As Spirit we again encounter God without form, directing and inspiring us upon our spiritual path.

As with God the Father, the breath, the wind, the Spirit moving there in the open space is, in fact, the divine energy moving through the space of our consciousness. And again, if we have begun to let go of our story and all other so-called belongings, we may be able to feel the Spirit moving us. If we are tied to our imaginary self, however, and live in our story about that, if we are tied to the people and things that "belong" to us, we cannot experience the Spirit. *It is easier for a camel to go through the eye of a needle than for someone who is rich [in possessions] to enter the kingdom of God.*[37]

Faith in no-thing

At this point we have an opportunity to deepen our grasp of faith in God. Clearly it can no longer be a loyalty to our favorite scripture passages. Nor can it be having the correct mental beliefs directed at an imagined God in the sky. Rather, faith now looks more like a trust in the empty, spacious awareness that belongs to God, and is God. So instead of trusting in ourselves, in the *story of I,* to decide our next action, we can now have faith in God's spaciousness. Here everything appears, here everything is loved, and here we can wait for God to direct us. We have faith in no-thing.

a contemplative path to God

You find out

> Explore your experience of God without form: While praying, notice where the God to whom you pray is located. Do you find a location for God without form? Then quietly turn your mind toward someone who is ill or bereaved. As you begin to experience some feeling and compassion for them, what does that compassionate Spirit look like? Does it have a size, a color, a shape?

10
FULFILLMENT & EMPTINESS

How Do I Love?

We see God's love for us revealed through the life, death, and resurrection of Jesus. Out of the experience of God's forgiving love we find that we have love to share with others. *We love because he first loved us.*[38] We cultivate the loving presence of God in our hearts and minds.

A story that may be denied

In contemplative experience, we find that in order to become full of God's love, one must become empty of self. Indeed, the more that we experience our self as simply a story, the more we see how insubstantial our self is and how open and empty we truly are. Jesus put it this way:

> *If any want to become my followers, let them deny themselves and take up their cross daily and follow me. For those who want to save their life will lose it, and those who lose their life for my sake will save it.*[39]

The more our "self" is revealed as a story that may be denied, the more we can see that our true nature is simply awareness, the space in which appear our thoughts, our stories, and everything else.

Love is the characteristic quality of this selfless awareness. Compassion is what this awareness is and does. This Godly love does not need to be urged upon us or taken as an obligation. It flows from selfless awareness as effortlessly as water flows from a spring. In fact: *Life is love flowing out of emptiness.*[40] However, if my consciousness is full of concern, say, for my becoming a loving person, there is little room for my neighbor or for love. *Those who try to make their life secure will lose it, but those who lose their life will keep it.*[41]

Becoming the neighbor

Richard Rohr maintains that we take the path inward to find our true self in God; and we discover that the very same path has led us out into the midst of the world.[42] Freed from the myopia caused by living within our own *story of I*, we begin to appreciate the strange, wondrous people and things around us, as if for the first time. Our relationships are transformed when we begin to live as awareness, when awareness is all that we are. The physical bodies of our friends appear in our visual awareness—that is, in us. Their voices arise in our auditory awareness, in us. We can see parts of their *stories of I* in our mental awareness. How natural, how simple it is to listen to them, to have love and compassion for them. To rephrase Walt Kelly's possum, Pogo: "We have met the others, and they is us." We see familiar family and friends with fresh regard. *You shall love your neighbor as yourself.*[43]

Ironically, our so-called enemies can help us on our path in a way that our friends cannot. We feel negativity and aversion for an "enemy." These little feelings of suffering give us a fresh look at where we are clinging to something, where we are causing ourselves suffering, where we can let go and become the compassionate awareness that we really are. For this reason it can be said that our enemies are our best spiritual teachers. They expose the places where we are clinging and grasping for our selves. These places will seldom appear when we are with comfortable friends.

My story like a puppy

We should note that our *story of I* is still here. It has been spinning since we were small children, and it has become a deeply ingrained, habitual way of thinking. However, now that we can see clearly that it is only a story, we can keep an eye on it. And we don't have to believe everything it tells us anymore. It tags along with us like a puppy dog on a leash. The puppy keeps tugging this way and that, throwing out thoughts, opinions, ideas,

a contemplative path to God

objections, and proposals. We can take note of these tugs without being completely drawn into our *story of I* as we used to be. This puppy is a conditioned, habit-driven thing. It will always run for something delicious to eat. It will always try to avoid discomfort and pain. It is pretty predictable. Our story is composed of all our self-centeredness: our personality, our likes and dislikes, our habitual thoughts and fantasies, our ingrained habits and neuroses, our prejudices and unconscious biases. Our *story of I* is still with us on the path, even though we are no longer feeding it with a lot of strong opinions and important dislikes.

The tie that does not bind

When we are drawn more fully into union with God (see the next two chapters), the "I" finally disappears from the story. The sages say it becomes like a rope which has been placed in a fire and burned. The ashes still have the shape of a rope, but it no longer has the power to bind anything. Note that our conditioning and training remain, but are no longer tied to "I" at the center.

In the service of God, rather than in service of our self-centeredness, our conditioning is an immense help. It includes being able to speak our native language, find the way home, remember what we planned to do today—all of the needful habits and knowledge that we depend upon in daily life. We would be hard-pressed to express love and compassion without them. So for the time being we just need to keep seeing our story for the self-centered, mechanical thing that it is. We do not want to be pulled off the contemplative path and back into the bramble bushes of actually believing in our *story of I* again.

A work of art

Perhaps we are now ready to appreciate our story in a new way. Our wordy story is a conditioned thing. Now that we have seen it for what it is, it has little power to deceive us with its "reality" or envelop us with its anxieties. Our own *story of I* can now evoke the same compassion that is becoming natural for us to give to others. Here is another illustration adapted from Huston Smith's

a contemplative path to God

The World's Religions: In the dentist's chair our *story of I* begins to fret about discomfort and pain. Then we hear our spacious awareness say calmly, "It's okay. You'll only be here for a little while. Soon it will all be over."

From the perspective of awareness we can see our story as the creative fabrication, even work of art, that it is. We now become free to *consciously* create a new, appropriate story for each situation. For a couple of hours I live the story of a loving husband, then I create a new story of a social activist as I work on selling wreaths made by farm worker women. Such stories are necessary to focus and express my love. Yet I see that the story remains a story. I temporarily mistake it for a self now and again, just as I mistake the patches of colored light on a movie screen for real people. But later on I notice, "Oh, that's just a story."

Contemplative teacher Cynthia Bourgeault has a wonderful analogy for the relation between our egoic self and our true self. She says that our true self in God uses the egoic self *as a useful instrument of manifestation—in the same way a violin lets you manifest the music. But you have come to know you are not your violin.*[44]

Imaginary people

Some will object that if our *stories of I* have no more substance than the characters on a movie screen, how can we have love or compassion for them? Why bother with all these imaginary people? The answer is that these people are—as we will see more clearly in the next chapter—manifestations of God, art forms created by our Lord. When we meet our neighbor we encounter Jesus, as Mother Teresa took pains to teach us. They are suffering beings, as we are or were, and they are part and parcel of our very own awareness. *Truly I tell you, just as you did it to one of the least of these who are members of my family, you did it to me.*[45]

All one whole

Contemplatives express compassion and love in making moral judgments and in working for justice in social affairs. They say that we must take a stand against the social expressions of the

a contemplative path to God

false self. However, they point out that all of our moral judgments are relative—that is, based upon comparisons. While we all may agree with the principle that lying is wrong, when one is lying to the gang members in order to protect the young boy hiding in the basement, lying is right. And indeed every moral decision requires that we ask the same question: Is this action right in relation to this situation?

We may base a judgment upon teachings in the Bible, and yet our judgment represents only our thought on how to apply what we have found —not the absolute truth of the matter. In fact, it is God alone who is absolute truth. So it is with considerable inner humility that the contemplative mounts the barricades to fight for a cause. For it could always turn out to be a mistake.

Serious or even violent conflicts over issues such as abortion show how difficult it can be to speak our sense of God's truth in a compassionate way. Rick Ufford-Chase, who has worked for years in a U.S.-Mexico border ministry, offers this practical way for us to dialogue with those with whom we differ. He says that we must keep two messages in our hearts: The first is "I love you," and the second, "I may be wrong."[46]

At the deepest level, contemplatives see all social conflict as tragic and needless suffering due to conflicting parties who have no idea that they are parts of one whole. Etty Hillesum was a Jew living amidst the terror of the Nazi-occupied Netherlands. She later worked tirelessly in a forced-work camp to ease the suffering of others. She was murdered at Auschwitz in 1943, at the age of 29. In the midst of terror, pain, persecution, and death, this young woman was able to make this contemplative witness:

> *It is all as one in me and I accept it all as one mighty whole and begin to grasp it better if only for myself, without being able to explain to anyone else how it all hangs together.*[47]

Compassionate love, after doing all that it can to alleviate the suffering around and within, gives

a contemplative path to God

itself up to the will of God, whose love cannot be quenched and whose gracious purpose cannot be overcome: *not my will but yours be done.*

You find out

> Use this experiment to investigate your own experience of loving: Visualize a needy person whom you find it difficult to love. Now imagine that you have become as selfless as the surrounding air. Like the space above a battlefield that remains completely unharmed by the fighting, you have nothing to fear from this person, nothing to lose or gain in relationship to him or her. Now, as this space of awareness, what is your attitude toward this difficult person?

11
MY SELF & DIVINE UNION

Where Is the Kingdom of God?

As Christians we all desire to live in God's kingdom. We want to feel the bliss and see the truth of God. Yet, often we do not feel God's presence, and it seems that God has withdrawn from us. At other times we may feel that it is we who have left God through breaking the commandments, through selfishness, or by simple forgetfulness.

Manifestations of the divine

Contemplatives have a fresh perspective upon God's presence. They emphasize that God has not forsaken us, and then, surprisingly, they go on to assert that neither have we left God. We are already in union with God, in the kingdom of God, but we are unaware of it. Jesus said, *Abide in me, as I abide in you.*[48] In other words, "Come to live within me, for I am already within you." We have already seen that we are each a space of awareness which is also the infinite space of God's awareness. It is out of the empty space of God that literally everything comes and to which it goes. We are all expressions of God. We need to see *the plight of our ignorance in which we go about as manifestations of the divine seeking union with the divine.*[49] For at the center of who we really are, we are forever united with God.

> *For I am convinced that neither death, nor life, nor angels, nor rulers, nor things present, nor things to come, nor powers, nor height, nor depth, nor anything else*

in all creation, will be able to separate us from the love of God in Christ Jesus our Lord.[50]

Christ's death, our death

When we can no longer escape the fact of our selflessness, our false self, the *story of I,* is finished: *We know that our old self was crucified with him so that the body of sin might be destroyed, and we might no longer be enslaved to sin.*[51] We begin to appreciate our Lord's selflessness from the inside. We glimpse how he could be so completely free as to give himself up completely. We see that his way of selflessness is the only way for us to finally escape our separation from God, that is, escape our sin.

Death is a very apt metaphor for what is happening here. Obviously, literal death is not implied, for Paul is alive as he writes about our old self being crucified with Christ. Spiritually, we can die before we die. We can die to the *story of I,* making it powerless to make itself the center of our vast, spiritual space. We can see that this false self is imaginary. This spiritual death, as we shall see, brings a reunion with human beings, a union with God, and the joy of heaven. Listen to Jesus once more: *Unless a grain of wheat falls into the earth and dies, it remains just a single grain; but if it dies, it bears much fruit.*[52]

Perfectly real

When contemplatives see experientially that they are one with God, they can look back upon their lives and see that this had always been the case. However, like most of us, they had not experienced this divine union earlier because they had accepted their thoughts as more real than what was right there all along. *The peace that passes understanding*, our true happiness, has been right here within us. But, preoccupied with our thought, we overlook it. At every moment, as Jesus proclaims, *the kingdom of God is at hand.*[53] It is here, it is the real, directly in front of us. We have only to be open to receive it. Why not behold what is, rather than be trapped in our swirl of outworn thoughts about what is?

In divine union we can see the perfection of

a contemplative path to God

the kingdom of heaven. But it is not perfection according to my values and criteria. Rather, the perfection of the kingdom appears when I let go of all my judgments in order to gratefully receive what is actually here in awareness.

View from the inside

A student came to his spiritual teacher with this question: "Is there any difference between the world that you live in and the world I live in?" His teacher replied, "No, it is exactly the same world, but for you it is outside, and for me it is inside." That is: "For you it is outside the body you think you are. And for me it is inside the consciousness I see that I am."

If you set your personal agenda aside for a few moments, and actually look, you may be able to see that the world is indeed inside your open space of awareness: right now, perhaps, assorted furniture, walls, electric lights, your body, and these pages. No one else is aware of these things at exactly the angle, with exactly the lighting, as you are. In a few minutes you will get up and walk and some objects will disappear and others arise. But while every object comes and goes, the vast empty space of your awareness remains the same.

As you observe this space, your direct experience is that you are precisely this continuing space of awareness wherein all sights, sounds, sensations, and thoughts appear and disappear. This open spaciousness is the no-thing of God, who is emphatically not a thing. This spaciousness is the kingdom of God, our true nature. The trinity is here: At center we are an empty field of awareness in divine union with the empty field of God. So also, our bodies are the body of Christ in the world, so that we can physically carry and implement his love. And we can sense the energy of the Spirit of love gently shifting within our awareness, guiding us toward others who need compassion.

All as divine

In union with God, we can begin to appreciate that everything we see is taking place in the spaciousness of divine union and, in that sense, is a manifestation of God. Finley calls this *the divinity of what just is.*[54] Listen to Paul's declaration: *Ever since the creation of the world [God's] eternal power and divine nature, invisible though they are, have been understood and seen through the things he has made.*[55] Everything we perceive is a form of consciousness, whether it seems good or bad, wonderful or terrible. Job points toward this when he says, *Shall we receive the good at the hand of God, and not receive the bad?*[56] And Jesus called his impending arrest a "betrayal" and threw himself on the ground to pray, *My Father, if it is possible, let this cup pass from me.* But he also saw that his arrest could be a manifestation of God: *Yet not what I want but what you want.*[57]

As each event arises in our clear, spacious awareness, it stands before us as an awareness of sound, movement, color, and so on. Then it disappears back into clear awareness. All events and objects are forms of the spacious awareness which is divine union. Thus there can be no union with God that is not simultaneously a union with all others. No wonder love for others arises so spontaneously from divine union. As Meister Eckhart put it,

> *The [one] who has God essentially present to him grasps God divinely, and to him God shines in all things; for everything tastes to him of God, and God forms himself for the man out of all things.*[58]

Cynthia Bourgeault speaks of this as being *like light pouring through a stained glass window*. Unity and diversity can be seen at once.[59]

Everything from God

When we directly experience divine union with our whole heart, even for a short while, we can receive everything that comes to us as coming directly from God. Hidden grudges against what God has given us tend to dissolve. We start to become reconciled to God in every specific detail of our life. 20th century mystic Simone Weil tells us how we can learn to receive everything as from God:

> *It is to know, with our whole soul and not just abstractly, that men who are*

not animated by pure charity are merely wheels in the mechanism of the order of the world, like inert matter. After that we see that everything comes directly from God, either through the love of man, or through the lifelessness of matter.[60]

Waves on the ocean

Here is an ancient metaphor for our divine union with God: Before the beginning, there was only the great, cosmic ocean that was God. It was smoother than glass, entirely calm and peaceful. Then God caused small bumps of water to appear on the surface. Each bump knew that it was simply the water of God in form. But after some time the taller bumps began to look around at the other bumps and identify themselves as individuals. They said, "We are waves!" They gathered together to find out who was taller or bigger or faster. Soon arguments broke out, fights ensued, and wars began to be planned. They had completely forgotten their true nature as the water of God. But they could never, ever, be anything except that.

You find out

Take a few moments to look at your own spacious awareness: Notice the *story of I* running along in your mind. Now turn your attention toward the empty physical space within which you are sitting. How is this emptiness different from the emptiness in the next room? Outside this building? Now relax as your own space of awareness. Where is the boundary between your empty spaciousness and God's?

12
PRACTICE & GRACE

How Do I Walk This Path?

It is not necessary to understand any of the preceding explanation in order to walk or practice the contemplative path. We have reviewed the contemplative story to this point in hope of satisfying our rationality that this path "makes sense." Otherwise our thinking mind may rebel and refuse to allow us to walk the path, saying: "Why am I doing this? What is the reason for that? You are wasting my time!"

Authentic contemplative teachers will advise you that this path consists of your own practice, your own spiritual work. They will insist that you not take their word for anything: "If you try to believe me, you will end up with only thoughts and no experience of the reality to which my teachings point, as a finger points. Go and practice these teachings, experiment like a scientist, test for yourself whether or not what I have told you is true." Each time that you performed (not just read) one of the *You find out* exercises in this book, you placed a foot upon the path.

Simple but not easy

In actuality the contemplative path is so simple that it can be pointed to by a single word. It is *selflessness*, the realization that you do not have an individual self. Or, it may be called *poverty*, the recognition that you do not possess anything at all. Again, it is *awareness*, the discovery that you are consciousness itself. It is the path toward the total realization that selves are imaginary, that there is simply awareness in God.

a contemplative path to God

However, this simple path is not easy: *For the gate is narrow and the road is hard that leads to life, and there are few who find it.*[61] It requires that we let go of all that we have. *The kingdom of heaven is like treasure hidden in a field, which someone found and hid; then in his joy he goes and sells all that he has and buys that field.*[62] Yet the promise is that the path need not be a burden. *For my yoke is easy, and my burden is light.*[63]

To walk this path is simply to practice living in awareness of our union with God. Reading about spirituality, thinking, talking—words, words, words—will not be enough. Like road signs, words can point where to go, but they cannot take you there. Remember that Jesus is the word made flesh, not the word made into still more words again. As he says in Luke's gospel, *Why do you call me 'Lord, Lord,' and do not do what I tell you?*[64] In other words, practice. Contemplative practices are performed so as to release our identification with any thought (we are not thoughts) and with any thing (we are not things) so that we come to rest as the empty space of awareness that we are, which belongs to God.

Almost any activity may become a spiritual practice: gardening, writing poetry, skiing, painting, hiking. Of course we will want to complement such activities with one or more of the traditional practices, which we will discuss in a moment. Whatever the activity, it must be found to bring us in touch with the One whom we seek. James Finley puts it this way:

> *A contemplative practice is any act, habitually entered into with your whole heart, as a way of awakening, deepening and sustaining a contemplative experience of the inherent holiness of the present moment.*[65]

Compassion above all

There is one practice that is so all-inclusive that it inevitably appears before, after, and within all the others. This is the practice of love and compassion. Perhaps we do not so much practice this as we simply learn to observe it. For it is God's

a contemplative path to God

love, flowing of itself out of selflessness, poverty and awareness. It is our place to yield ourselves up into that flowing. When we must decide between responding to the call of love and compassion or doing some other practice, love will always win if we are true to our selflessness and our poverty.

Historically, the formal practices of the contemplative path may be divided into four broad approaches: morality, devotion, meditation, and inquiry. Most seekers who travel the path as described here will emphasize meditation.

Morality

Morality, the first type of practice, can play a unique role on this spiritual path. In addition to using moral values in making ethical choices, we can use morality to discover where we are attempting to cling to something and possess it. Using the Ten Commandments or perhaps a set of moral precepts drawn up by a spiritual community, this practice is to pay special attention when we begin to violate a particular precept. For example, suppose you are filling out a form and are about to falsify a few numbers. You pause as you realize that these are not honest numbers. "What am I clinging to that makes me want to be dishonest here?," you ask. "Oh, I am protecting my bank account, I am clinging to my money." Then you can see that you are all worried and tense about something that cannot bring lasting happiness: an impermanent bank account. As you relax your clinging to it, you relax your suffering, and are at last ready to deal with filling out the form. The more such possessions we let go of, the smaller our possessive little *story of I* becomes, and the easier it is to see the here and now of God.

Devotion

Such practice in letting go of things can help us enter the second practice, devotion. This is the practice of surrendering to God all that we are, in prayer, worship, and daily living. *You shall love the Lord your God with all your heart, and with all your soul, and with all your mind, and with all your strength.*[66] In this love for the divine we give up all we have been, all we think we are, and all our dreams for tomorrow. We seek to dramatize in ritual and actualize in practice a complete selflessness, wherein we continually ask that *not my will but yours be done*. As Meister Eckhart explains:

> *There should be a pure going out from what is yours. And therefore in the best of all prayers that [one] can pray, there should not be 'Give me this virtue, or that way of life,' or 'Yes, Lord, give me yourself, or give me everlasting life,' but 'Lord, give me nothing but what you will, and do, Lord, whatever and however you will in every way.'* [67]

Meditation

Such deep devotion to God is an excellent place from which to begin the next practice, meditation. Sometimes called "contemplation," "the prayer of silence," or "centering prayer," meditation is the most widely used contemplative practice. It may be viewed as a form of silent prayer or communion with God. Although we have used it more broadly in this book, the word "contemplation" is sometimes reserved to describe the contemplative experience of God that is completely beyond any practice—directly given by God.

There are two broad contemporary movements in the church that place great emphasis upon meditation: Contemplative Outreach, led by Father Thomas Keating, and the World Community for Christian Meditation, led by Laurence Freeman, OSB. Both teach meditation as a daily practice for the contemplative path.

Formal meditation practice ordinarily involves sitting on the floor or on a chair for a period of 20 to 40 minutes or so. Usually one focuses the attention upon some object: the breath, a repeated prayer, or a religious object. We quickly find out how difficult this simple practice can be as our minds dart away from the object, into thoughts. However, when meditation is practiced regularly over a period of time, the mind can learn to keep its attention more and more upon the object. Then we have the opportunity to see reality itself without being immediately distracted by our thoughts about it. Meditation is practice in realizing our union with God, for it opens us to the spacious awareness that we are. Father Keating has humorously but accurately referred to it as *taking a little vacation from your self.*[68]

Inquiry

In meditation practice we learn to focus our attention. Such a disciplined, focused attention enables the fourth practice: inquiry. Inquiry involves both the study of teachings and the study of ourselves. First, we study spiritual teachings in order to clarify the path, to inspire our life in faith, and to find instruction in contemplative practices. Then we turn to study ourselves to find out, firsthand, *who am I?* This book has been presenting the contemplative path from the point of view of inquiry. Suggestions for inquiry practice can be found throughout the book, and especially in the *You find out* exercises.

Here is an example of another inquiry practice, very simple but very deep:

> *Instead of simply taking for granted what we have been taught about the nature of ourselves and the world, we begin to pay attention to our actual experience. For example, whatever arises in Consciousness—be it a thought, feeling, sensation, emotion, or an impulse of will—we might inquire: Is this phenomenon me, or not-me?*[69]

We can then look to see if we can find the boundaries that make these things part of "me." By practicing this and similar inquiries day after day, we can begin to see in our direct experience the difference between the transitory things and people of the world, and the continuing awareness—our true nature—in which the world appears.

Turning failure into practice

Inevitably, you will experience frustrations as you enter into a spiritual practice. You will try in meditation, for example, to follow ten breaths with your attention, and your mind will wonder off into a train of thought after three. Or you will be

a contemplative path to God

unable to find out why you want to violate a moral precept. When this happens and you find yourself saying, "Why can't I do this?" look and see that this frustration is only a thought accompanied by some tension in your body. Allow the thought to dissolve and the stress will subside. By releasing the thought, you have already returned to your practice. You have become an awareness of things as they are and perhaps you have glimpsed divine union: For God identifies with us in our frustration, in and as our own compassionate love for our imperfect self.[70]

Grace

We do not grow spiritually on this path. In fact, all our spiritual practices must eventually end in failure. They aim at divine union yet we cannot enter that union by our own will. This is largely due to the fact that when we practice, it is our egoic self, our *story of I*, that is concerned to succeed. So whether we judge that we are doing well or badly with a particular practice, our separate, egoic self is going to be strengthened by such judgments (see chapter 7). The solution for this "catch 22" lies in letting go of our judgments and allowing God's grace to lead us into:

> *a self-transforming path of an ever deeper, more expansive acceptance of ever deeper, more expansive levels of our powerlessness to be anything other than the way we simply are, one with the way the present moment simply is.*[71]

Nonetheless, with regular practice we can become more and more aware of our *story of I* as just a collection of thoughts. This is part of what it means to be crucified with Christ: to see our false self, more and more, as purely a product of imagination. But as we near the end of the path only the grace of God can help us. For when we are almost there, when our egoic self is fruitlessly struggling to lay itself down before God, God alone can raise us up with Christ into divine union: *Therefore we have been buried with him by baptism into death, so that, just as Christ was raised from the dead by the glory of the Father, so we too might walk in newness of life.*[72]

Setting out upon the path

If we are attracted to this path but do not actually walk it, we are likely to be *merely wheels in the mechanism of the order of the world, like inert matter.* Thoughts about it will not take you anywhere. You must step out onto the path.

It is common in spiritual circles to stress three components of walking a contemplative path: teacher, community, and practice. A teacher helps us see the path and leads us back when we unknowingly step off. A good teacher can show us where we are actually practicing suffering when we think we are practicing divine union. Although one may begin the contemplative path by reading books and listening to tapes or videos of teachers, there is really no substitute for the inspiration and instruction of a flesh-and-blood contemplative teacher. A careful search of Protestant and Catholic resources in your community will likely uncover a spiritual teacher who can guide you on this path.

A contemplative community can encourage and support our practice. We can practice together and feel the power of joint intention. We can confide our problems and share our insights on the path. We can practice showing love and compassion in a setting of understanding and acceptance.

The end of the path

The spiritual path has a beginning in suffering and an end in divine union. For a very few, the path seems to be only a matter of days. Most of the rest of us who choose this path will practice for months or years or perhaps decades. This could amount to a lot of practice. But what is the alternative? Do we really want to go back to a mechanical life in which we are enslaved to our habitual little *story of I* and spend the rest of our lives trying to make that imaginary self feel a bit better?

The contemplative path lies in front of us. It proceeds directly into the kingdom of God and the world. It is the path of selflessness, poverty and awareness. It begins with the simple desire to find abiding happiness, which no impermanent person

a contemplative path to God

or thing can provide. As we enter into practice, we will be amazed to begin to notice the difference between our direct experience of things and our blinding flurry of thoughts about them. We will start to feel a joyful relief as we discover that our all-important self looks more and more like just a story. With awe we will have glimpses of ourselves as open, spacious awareness. Without any effort, we will find ourselves opening to a fresh compassion for those who are in pain and suffering. As spaciousness, we will realize that our individual, egoic self is finally in ashes. We are in union with our Happiness, our God, forever.

> *I have been crucified with Christ*
> *and it is no longer I who live*
> *but it is Christ who lives in me.*[73]

Notes

1. John W. Groff, Jr., *The Smell of Incense, Sound of Silence* (Cincinnati: Forward Movement Publications, 1988) 20.

2. Cynthia Bourgeault, *Centering Prayer and Inner Awakening* (Cambridge, MA: Cowley Publications, 2004) 5.

3. Thomas Merton, *New Seeds of Contemplation* (New York: New Directions Publishing, 1972) 1.

4. Mark 2.17.

5. Matthew 19.23.

6. I Corinthians 3.16.

7. Quoted in *John of the Cross: Selected Writings*, ed. Kieran Kavanaugh O.C.D. (New York: Paulist Press, 1987) 191.

8. *The Cloud of Unknowing*, ed. James Walsh, S.J. (New York: Paulist Press, 1981) 103.

9. Anthony de Mello, *Awakening* (Chicago: Loyola Press, 1998) 151.

10. John 3.11.

11. James 2.17.

12. James Finley, *The Contemplative Heart* (Notre Dame, Indiana: Sorin Books, 2000) 92-93.

13. Matthew 6.19.

14. Psalms 103.15f.

15. Anthony de Mello, *The Way to Love* (New York: Doubleday, 1991) 162.

16. Philippians 3.8.

17. *John of the Cross: Selected Writings,* ed. Kieran Kavanaugh O.C.D., 66.

18. St. Teresa of Avila, *Interior Castle*, trans. E. Allison Peers (New York: Image Books, 1961) 9.

19. Merton, *New Seeds of Contemplation,* 35.

NOTES

20. This phrase was created by Joel Morwood, Spiritual Director of the Center for Sacred Sciences, in Eugene, Oregon.

21. Merton, *New Seeds of Contemplation*, 34.

22. C. S. Lewis, "Two Facades," *Not of this World: A Treasury of Christian Mysticism*, ed. James S. Cutsinger (Bloomington, Indiana: World Wisdom, Inc., 2003) 164.

23. Quoted in *Mysticism*, Evelyn Underhill (New York: New American Library, 1974), 200. Catherine of Siena, who died at 33 years, left us her wonderful dialogues with God. A summary of Catherine's major writings may be found in *Catherine of Siena, The Dialogue*, trans. Suzanne Noffke, in the Classics of Western Spirituality series.

24. Romans 12.2.

25. John 17.22-23.

26. I Corinthians 12.27.

27. John 15.11.

28. Colossians 3.9-10.

29. Luke 12.20.

30. Luke 22.42.

31. Richard Rohr, *Simplicity, The Art of Living* (New York: Crossroad, 1991) 164.

32. Brother Lawrence of the Resurrection, *The Practice of the Presence of God*, trans. Salvatore Sciurba (Washington, D.C.: ICS Publications, 1994) 31.

33. Deuteronomy 5.8.

34. John 1.14.

35. I Corinthians 12.27.

36. John 3.8.

37. Mark 10.25.

38. I John 4.19.

39. Luke 9.23-24.

40. Joel Morwood. Talk given at Center for Sacred Sciences, in Eugene, Oregon.

41. Luke 17.33.

42. Rohr, *Simplicity*.

43. Mark 12.31.

NOTES

44. Bourgeault, *Centering Prayer*, 167.

45. Matthew 25.40.

46. Rick Ufford-Chase, Moderator, Presbyterian Church (USA), from a talk given April 29, 2005 at Central Presbyterian Church, in Eugene, Oregon.

47. Etty Hillesum, *An Unfinished Life* (New York: Washington Square Press, 1981) 130f.

48. John 15.4.

49. Finley, *Contemplative Heart*, 77.

50. Romans 8.38-39.

51. Romans 6.6.

52. John 12.24.

53. Mark 1.15.

54. Finley, *Contemplative Heart*, 19.

55. Romans 1.20.

56. Job 2.10.

57. Matthew 26.39.

58. Meister Eckhart, *Everything As Divine: The Wis-*

dom of Meister Eckhart, trans. Edmund Ciolledge, O.S.A., and Bernard McGinn. ed. Stephen J. Connor (New York: Paulist Press, 1996) 35.

59. Bourgeault, *Centering Prayer*.

60. Simone Weil, *Waiting for God*, trans. Emma Craufurd (New York: Harper & Row, 1973) 157.

61. Matthew 7.14.

62. Matthew 13.44.

63. Matthew 11.30.

64. Luke 6.46.

65. Finley, *Contemplative Heart*, 46.

66. Mark 12.30.

67. Eckhart, *Everything is Divine*, 25-26.

68. Bourgeault, *Centering Prayer*, 19.

69. Joel Morwood, "Practices," article on website, Center for Sacred Sciences, February 24, 2004, www.centerforsacredsciences.org/practices.html#practices

70. Finley, *Contemplative Heart*, 164.

71. Finley, *Contemplative Heart*, 193.

Notes

72. Romans 6.4.
73. Galations 2.19-20.

Bibliography

For the sake of simplicity this book has limited itself to Christian teachers of the contemplative path. But there are abundant parallel contemplative (mystical) teachings in the other great religious traditions. Although the belief systems of some religions may include ideas that we find strange or even incomprehensible, many of their suggestions for spiritual practice can be extremely relevant for our Christian path. Here are some places where you might begin to explore:

Buddhist: Pema Chodron or Joseph Goldstein.

Hindu: Swami Prabhavananda, *The Sermon on the Mount.*

Jewish: Green & Holtz, *Your Word is Fire*.

Muslim Sufi: the poetry of Rumi or Hafiz.

> (Note: Some web sites listed below may have changed since the publication of this book.)

Bourgeault, Cynthia. *Centering Prayer and Inner Awakening*. Cambridge, MA: Cowley Publications, 2004. Dr. Bourgeault is a contemporary contemplative teacher. In scholarly yet clear prose, she provides not only a manual on centering prayer meditation but also vital teachings on the spiritual path. For information on Bourgeault's center in Victoria, B.C. go to www.contemplative.org

Brother Lawrence of the Resurrection. *The Practice of the Presence of God*. Trans. Salvatore Sciurba. Washington, D.C.: ICS Publications, 1994. This is the famous short collection of writings by the contemplative who practiced in the monastery kitchen. For a brief biography of Brother Lawrence, go to www.carmelite.com/saints/lawrence.shtml

Center for Sacred Sciences. This is an excellent source for contemporary interfaith articles on the mystical path, with an emphasis upon inquiry. Access: www.centerforsacredsciences.org

Cutsinger, James S., Ed. *Not of this World: A Treasury of Christian Mysticism*. Bloomington, Indiana: World Wisdom, Inc., 2003. This sampler of writings from exemplary contemplatives across the centuries is of varying difficulty.

De Mello, Anthony. *Awakening*. Chicago: Loyola Press, 1998. Contemplative, psychologist, Jesuit, and native of India, de Mello has a deep understanding of what makes us tick. This book is a collection of very short stories and legends for awakening. Although accessible, it is to be pondered in the heart. De Mello's biography may be found at www.slu.edu/organizations/wgsc/index.html

De Mello, Anthony. *The Way to Love*. New York: Doubleday, 1991. This is a great introduction to the irreplaceable practice of letting go. This compact book is very direct, accessible, conversational.

Eckhart, Meister. *Everything is Divine: The Wisdom of Meister Eckhart*. Trans. Edmund Ciolledge, O.S.A., and Bernard McGinn. Ed. Stephen J. Connor. New York: Paulist Press, 1996. Eckhart is one of the greatest masters of the Christian contemplative path. Here is a deceptively tiny book with excerpts from sermons and letters. This book is deep; you may need a teacher to get started in his work. A brief biography may be found at www.eckhartsociety.org/meister.htm

Edwards, Tilden. *Living in the Presence: Spiritual Exercises to Open Your Life to the Awareness of God*. New York: HarperCollins, 1995. A carefully contexted manual of exercises, this book contains a section on supporting spiritual practice in small groups. Edwards is quite accessible. For information on Dr. Edward's institute go to www.shalem.org

Finley, James. *The Contemplative Heart*. Notre Dame, Indiana: Sorin Books, 2000. A former student of Thomas Merton, Finley has a wonderful facility for showing the reader how to see into contemplative paradoxes. With unusual depth, the book is readable and rewarding.

Fox, Matthew. *Meditations with Meister Eckhart*. Santa Fe, New Mexico: Bear & Company, 1983. A good, brief introduction to both Meister Eckhart and Matthew Fox. Fox provides a framework for understanding excerpts from Eckhart's writings. Accessible with a little effort.

Harding, Douglas. *Trial of the Man Who Thought He Was God*. London: Penguin Group, 1992. Harding has unusual ways of demonstrating the simple reality of the path. The book is very accessible, but some will prefer to overlook the obvious. Find suggested experiments and more information at www.headless.org

Hillesum, Etty. *An Interrupted Life*. New York: Washington Square Press, 1981. This is a series of diary excerpts written by a young Jewish woman in Netherlands during the German occupation, World War II. She offers some amazing insights. More on Etty can be found at www.ehoc.ugent.be/index.php?id=80&type=content

Johnston, William, Ed. *The Cloud of Unknowing*. New York: Doubleday, 1973. This little book by an unknown 12th-century monk is one of the classic Christian contemplative texts. Johnston's editing makes this version accessible for the modern reader.

Kavanaugh, Kieran, OCD. Transl. *John of the Cross: Selected Writings*. New York: Paulist Press, 1987. John is perhaps the most celebrated contemplative in the church. Most of us will recall hearing of his "dark night of the soul." Most will do well to study this with a teacher or a commentary. For a short biography of John go to http://elvis.rowan.edu/~kilroy/JEK/12/14.html

Keating, Fr. Thomas. *Open Mind, Open Heart, The Contemplative Dimension of the Gospel*. Rockport, Maine: Element Books, 1991. This is a modern classic. Father Keating provides both historical background and practical meditation instruction in this slim volume. It is an accessible and thorough introduction to the centering prayer form of meditation. For information about the meditative movement led by Fr. Keating, go to www.centeringprayer.com

Main, John. *The Way of Unknowing, Expanding Spiritual Horizons Through Meditation*. New York: Crossroad, 1989. This book is comprised of thirty-nine brief talks originally given to a weekly meditation group in Montreal. Main taught a form of meditation using a repeated prayer or mantra. This accessible book contains practical contexts and advice. Learn about the meditation community started by John Main at www.wccm.org

Merton, Thomas. *New Seeds of Contemplation*. New York: New Directions Publishing, 1972. Merton was the most well-known contemplative of our time and wrote a host of books. This book is accessible despite being full of astonishing statements of spiritual insight that will make you stop and wonder.

Rohr, Richard. *Simplicity, The Art of Living*. New York: Crossroad, 1991. A well-known American Franciscan, Rohr was invited to Germany to give this series of talks on the spiritual life. In direct, unvarnished language, Rohr invites us to see the relation between our inward journey and our outward social responsibility. Quite readable. A new edition was published in 2003 entitled *Simplicity, The Freedom of Letting Go*. For information on Rohr's spiritual community, go to www.cacradicalgrace.org

St. Teresa of Avila. *Interior Castle*. Trans. E. Allison Peers. New York: Doubleday, 1961. Another great historic contemplative, a contemporary and mentor of St. John of the Cross. This book is difficult and may require a teacher's help. Teresa's biography may be found at www.karmel.at/eng/teresa.htm

Tuoti, Frank X. *Why Not Be a Mystic?* New York: Crosssroad Publishing Company, 1995. A former Trappist monk and student of Thomas Merton, Touti gives a thorough description of the path, drawing especially upon St. John of the Cross in addition to Merton. Of medium difficulty, this book is quite readable.

Weil, Simone. *Waiting for God*. Trans. Emma Craufurd. New York: Harper & Row, 1973. A radical, solitary thinker, Weil reveals unforgettable insights in this book of moderate difficulty. You may read her biography at www.kirjasto.sci.fi/weil.htm

Wesley Lachman is a practicing contemplative. He graduated with a B.A. in Psychology from Stanford University and a B.D. in Theology from San Francisco Theological Seminary. A retired minister in the Presbyterian Church (U.S.A.), he teaches spirituality at Central Presbyterian Church in Eugene, Oregon, and is active in social concerns. He studies the contemplative path at the Center for Sacred Sciences, an interfaith spiritual center in Eugene. He and his wife Sharry have two daughters and three grandchildren.

Your comments and questions regarding *The Shortest Way Home* are most welcome. Contact the author in care of the address below or at lachman@comcast.net by including the word "book" in the subject line of your e-mail.

Copies may be obtained online from amazon.com or through your local bookseller. You may also order direct from O Street Publishing for $10.95 plus $3.00 cost of mailing. For quantity orders, please inquire.

O Street Publishing
3534 High Street
Eugene, Oregon 97405
ostreetpublishing.com